ABOUT ISLAND PRESS

Island Press is the only nonprofit organization in the United States whose principal purpose is the publication of books on environmental issues and natural resource management. We provide solutions-oriented information to professionals, public officials, business and community leaders, and concerned citizens who are shaping responses to environmental problems.

In 2003, Island Press celebrates its nineteenth anniversary as the leading provider of timely and practical books that take a multidisciplinary approach to critical environmental concerns. Our growing list of titles reflects our commitment to bringing the best of an expanding body of literature to the environmental community throughout North America and the world.

Support for Island Press is provided by The Nathan Cummings Foundation, Geraldine R. Dodge Foundation, Doris Duke Charitable Foundation, Educational Foundation of America, The Charles Engelhard Foundation, The Ford Foundation, The George Gund Foundation, The Vira I. Heinz Endowment, The William and Flora Hewlett Foundation, Henry Luce Foundation, The John D. and Catherine T. MacArthur Foundation, The Andrew W. Mellon Foundation, The Moriah Fund, The Curtis and Edith Munson Foundation, National Fish and Wildlife Foundation, The New-Land Foundation, Oak Foundation, The Overbrook Foundation, The David and Lucile Packard Foundation, The Pew Charitable Trusts, The Rockefeller Foundation, The Winslow Foundation, and other generous donors.

The opinions expressed in this book are those of the author(s) and do not necessarily reflect the views of these foundations.

ABOUT THE LANDSCAPE ARCHITECTURE FOUNDATION

The Landscape Architecture Foundation is a national nonprofit organization whose mission is the preservation, improvement, and enhancement of the environment. LAF accomplishes its mission through information, research, and scholarship on landscape planning and design. LAF is leading a collaborative effort to improve the American environment through three interrelated programs— the *Land and Community Design Case Study Series*, the *Landscape Futures Initiative*, and the *National Center for Landscape Intervention*. These programs are designed to assist the landscape planning and design professions in meeting the public's demand for safer, healthier, and more livable communities. LAF is the only professional organization that provides a vision and a plan to meet the needs and identify the trends in landscape planning in the twenty-first century.

ABOUT THE LAND AND COMMUNITY DESIGN CASE STUDY SERIES

The Landscape Architecture Foundation's *Land and Community Design Case Studies* are a series of analytical publications by contemporary scholars and practitioners about topical issues and actual places in which design offers holistic solutions to economic, social, and environmental challenges. The goal of the series is to provide a legacy of critical thinking that will advance enlightened planning and development in the classroom, in practice and in policy.

CASE STUDY IN LAND AND COMMUNITY DESIGN

URBAN OPEN SPACE

DESIGNING FOR USER NEEDS

CASE STUDY IN LAND AND COMMUNITY DESIGN

URBAN OPEN SPACE

DESIGNING FOR USER NEEDS

MARK FRANCIS

ISLAND PRESS

WASHINGTON • COVELO • LONDON

LANDSCAPE ARCHITECTURE FOUNDATION

ISLAND PRESS is a trademark of
The Center for Resource Economics.

Library of Congress Cataloging-in-Publication Data
Francis, Mark.
Urban open space : designing for user needs /
Mark Francis.
    p. com. — (Land and community design case
       study series ; 3)
    Includes bibliographical references and index.
    ISBN 1-55963-113-9 (pbk. : alk. paper)
        1. Landscape architecture—Case studies.
        2. Landscape design—Case studies.
        3. Open spaces—Case studies.
    I. Title. II. Series.
    SB472.F69 2003
    712'.5—dc22   12003007887
                                        CIP

British Cataloguing-in-Publication Data available

Book packaging by Academy Press

Book design by Gimga Group

Printed on recycled, acid-free paper

Manufactured in the United States of America
10 9 8 7 6 5 4 3 2 1

CONTENTS

FOREWORD

The magnitude of social and environmental problems has increased dramatically during the post-World War II decades. The economic engine that has driven uncontrolled development has often not been balanced by social, historical, aesthetic, or environmental concerns. Suburban development and new communities have replaced the rural landscape with retail boxes, six-lane roads are lined with parking lots and billboards, and fast-food restaurants sit next to historic buildings.

Design and planning can make a difference. In fact, the body of evidence in both the natural and built environments suggests that inspired design can make a significant improvement in the lives of people and the life of our planet. From the transformation of the grittiest urban centers to the conservation of the grandest expanse of public lands, Americans have accumulated an unparalleled record of achievement in the creation of landscapes that enrich the human spirit.

The power of planning and design to connect seemingly unrelated systems and resources lies at the heart of our ability to leave a sustainable imprint on the planet. This is a lasting legacy for future generations. From urban centers to national parks, from intercity greenways to neighborhood playgrounds, landscape planning and design is one of the most effective, economical, and valuable methods of holistically addressing such topical issues as clean water, transportation patterns, open space protection, and community planning.

In order to solve these increasingly complex challenges, professionals and their clients need timely information on emerging issues and on innovative projects that show how and why certain approaches and schemes have been successful, as well as offer helpful criticism about their more problematic aspects. Information of this type is vital to the goals of protecting natural resources and landscapes, reclaiming disturbed lands, and creating sustainable communities that foster health and safety.

Such critical and multifaceted analyses and design, taking into account the land, history, society, economics, and land use regulations, can prevent many environmental, social, and health problems. It can also restore or improve degraded land and communities. Yet this requires planning and design of the highest quality. At the same time, high-quality design has become more difficult to achieve. Forces such as population migration and growth, and rapid urbanization, require landscape planners to assess each situation anew and bring fresh thinking, rather than old formulas, to the design of our living landscapes.

The Landscape Architecture Foundation is developing the *Land and Community Design Case Study Series* to meet this critical need. The series will enhance the skills and knowledge base of the landscape planning professions, inform public policy and land development decisions, and provide material for public education. The result will be the creation of environments with the capacity to restore and promote public welfare and health, as well as to protect and enhance the built and natural environments.

L. Susan Everett
Executive Director
Landscape Architecture Foundation
Washington, DC

URBAN OPEN SPACE

CASE STUDY IN LAND AND COMMUNITY DESIGN

The making of urban open space is a topic of considerable interest to landscape architects, their clients, and the public. Numerous studies have found that addressing user needs is a prerequisite to making good parks, plazas, and urban open spaces. User requirements in open space can include such varied considerations as comfort and relaxation, privatization of public space, reducing conflicts between hikers and dirt bikers, and dog versus human use of neighborhood parks. While considerable research has been done on needs and conflicts in open space, no single document integrates all of this knowledge and makes it available to professionals, students, and researchers. The purpose of this issue-based study is to review and synthesize this knowledge into an accessible and useful document. A related goal is to develop a prototype issue-based case study for the Landscape Architecture Foundation (LAF) to advance the development of future case studies.

OPPOSITE Bryant Park offers places for passive and active engagement.

It is hard to design a space that will not attract people.

What is remarkable is how often this has been accomplished.

—William Whyte,
"Revitalization of Bryant Park," 1979

INTRODUCTION
DESIGNING FOR USER NEEDS

Good management is critical to successful public open spaces.

OPPOSITE Use is an important prerequisite for successful public spaces.

Recently it has become more commonly understood that successful parks and open spaces such as plazas, streets, and public gardens are ones that are lively and well-used by people. The observations and writings of social scientists and designers such as William Whyte (1980, 1988), Clare Cooper Marcus (1970; and Wischemann 1987; and Francis 1998; and Barnes 1999), Kevin Lynch (1972, 1981), Jan Gehl (1987, 1996), Louise Mozingo (1989), Lyn Lofland (1998), and others have shown definitively that use is a requirement for good public landscapes. The purpose of this case study is to critically review this past research and make it accessible to students and practitioners.

In earlier work on public space, the architect Steve Carr, environmental psychologist Leanne Rivlin, planner Andrew Stone, and I proposed three broad dimensions of good open spaces: needs, rights, and meanings (Carr et al. 1992). In brief, we found that successful public spaces are ones that are responsive to the needs of their users; are democratic in their accessibility; and are meaningful for the larger community and society. The focus of this issue-based case study is to review and identify those critical user needs that must be considered in the planning, design, and management of outdoor spaces.[1]

1 / See *Public Space* (Carr et al. 1992) for a more comprehensive discussion of the dimensions that make good public spaces.

Many playgrounds such as this school roof play area are boring and dangerous.

Much design practice today lags behind research advances on the needs of people in public space. As a result, considerable problems and conflicts exist in urban public open space. These may occur between users and managers, designers and managers, or between different groups of users. We all know the problems in our own communities, such as playgrounds going unused, teenagers occupying spaces designed for the elderly, or conflicts between some park users and skateboarders, dirt bikers, or graffiti artists. While some of these conflicts are healthy and necessary tensions in urban public space, many serve as barriers to people enjoying places. Many conflicts can be reduced or even eliminated through effective programming, design, and management.

Research and case studies of a number of well-designed or redesigned public spaces offer evidence that user needs can be successfully provided for in urban parks, plazas, streets, and gardens. These include designs or redesigns of urban parks such as New York City's Bryant Park (Thompson 1997; Berens 1998; Francis 1999a) and Central Park (Carr et al. 1992); neighborhood spaces (Hester 1975; Brower 1988, 1996); and citywide park and open space systems (Longo 1996; Harnik 2000).

Playgrounds can be designed to be both playful and fun.

For the purposes of this case study, urban open space is defined as publicly accessible open spaces such as parks, plazas, streets, community gardens, and greenways (Carr et al. 1992; Lynch 1972). They include the spaces that Danish urban designer Jan Gehl (1987; Gehl and Gemoze 1996) has called "the life between buildings." They also are what the sociologist Ray Oldenburg (1989) calls "third places"—spaces that "host the regular, informal, and happily anticipated gatherings of individuals beyond the realms of home and work." A typology of urban open spaces is included in Table 1.

User needs are defined as those amenities and experiences that people seek in enjoying public open spaces. Needs provide the basic level of support and function in open space; they are the prerequisite for having an enjoyable landscape experience and provide the basis for much design criteria. They can range from the need for basic access to requirements for comfort and passive or active engagement. Put more simply, user needs may include the ability to walk into a space and find a comfortable place to sit and relax without being hassled.

User conflicts in public open spaces often emerge when user needs are not met, or from conflicts between different user groups. Conflicts may result from lack of access to a space reinforced by restrictive management or over-design. They can also occur when different users have competing purposes and meanings they attach to public open space. Examples include conflicts between users of different ages, sex, or cultural background. Other problems result from a lack of user involvement in the design and management of spaces. A deeper understanding of needs and conflicts can aid designers and managers in creating most successful public open spaces.

Many user needs can be designed into public open spaces. The Children's Fountain in Central Park, Davis, California.

TABLE 1

A Typology of Urban Open Spaces

Type/Subtype of Open Space	Characteristics
PUBLIC PARKS	
Public/Central Park	Publicly developed and managed open space as part of zoned open space system of city; open space of city-wide importance; often larger than neighborhood park.
Downtown Parks	Green parks with grass and trees located in downtown areas; can be traditional, historic parks or newly developed open spaces.
Commons	A large green area developed in older New England cities and towns; once pasture area for common use; now used for leisure activities.
Neighborhood Park	Open space developed in residential environments; publicly developed and managed as part of the zoned open space of cities, or as private residential development; may include playgrounds, sport facilities, etc.
Mini/Vestpocket Park	Small urban park bounded by buildings; may include fountain or water feature.
SQUARES AND PLAZAS	
Central Square	Square or plaza; often part of historic development of city center; may be formally planned or exist as meeting places of streets; frequently publicly developed and managed.
MEMORIALS	
	Public place that memorializes people or events of local and national importance.
MARKETS	
Farmers Markets	Open space or streets used for farmers markets or flea markets; often temporary or occur only during certain times in existing space such as parks, downtown streets or parking lots.
STREETS	
Pedestrian Sidewalks	Part of cities where people move on foot; most commonly sidewalks and paths, planned or found, which connect one destination with another.
Pedestrian Mall	Street closed to auto traffic; pedestrian amenities provided such as benches, plantings; often located along main street in downtown area.
Transit Mall	Development of improved transit access to downtown areas; replacement of traditional pedestrian malls with bus and "light rail" malls.
Traffic Restricted Streets	Streets used as public open space; traffic and vehicle restriction can include pedestrian improvements and sidewalk widening, street tree planting.
Town Trails	Connect parts of cities through integrated urban trails; use of streets and open spaces planned as setting for environmental learning; some are designed and marked trails.

PLAYGROUNDS

Playground	Play area located in neighborhood; frequently includes traditional play equipment such as slides and swings; sometimes includes amenities for adults such as benches; can also include innovative designs such as adventure playgrounds.
School yard	School yard as play area; some developed as place for environmental learning or as community use spaces.

COMMUNITY OPEN SPACES

Community Garden/Park	Neighborhood spaces designed, developed or managed by local residents on vacant land; may include viewing gardens, play areas, and community gardens; often developed on private land; not officially viewed as part of open space system of cities; often vulnerable to displacement by other uses such as housing and commercial development.

GREENWAYS AND LINEAR PARKWAYS

	Interconnected recreational and natural areas connected by pedestrian and bicycle paths.

URBAN WILDERNESS

	Undeveloped or wild natural areas in or near cities; often popular for hiking, dog walking and recreation; frequently involves conflicts between users and ecological preservation/restoration.

ATRIUM/INDOOR MARKETPLACES

Atrium	Interior private space developed as indoor atrium space; an indoor, lockable plaza or pedestrian street; counted by many cities as part of open space system; privately developed and managed as part of new office or commercial development.
Marketplace/Downtown Shopping Center	Interior, private shopping areas, usually freestanding or rehabilitation of older building(s); may include both interior and outdoor spaces; some times called "festival marketplaces"; privately developed and managed as part of new office or commercial development.

FOUND/NEIGHBORHOOD SPACES

Everyday Spaces	Publicly accessible open places such as street corners and steps to buildings, which people claim and use.
Neighborhood Spaces	Publicly accessible open space such as street corners and lots near where people live; can also be vacant or undeveloped space located in neighborhood including vacant lots and future building sites; often used by children, teenagers, and local residents.

WATERFRONTS

Waterfronts, Harbors, Beaches, Riverfronts, Piers, Lakefronts	Open space along waterways in cities; increased public access to water development of waterfront parks.

Source: Adapted from Carr et al. 1992.

A case study is a well-documented and systematic examination of the process, decision-making and outcomes of a landscape project or issue that can inform future practice, policy, theory and/or education.

—Mark Francis, "A Case Study Method for
Landscape Architecture," 1999

LAF CASE STUDY METHOD

This case study of designing for user needs in urban open spaces uses a method prepared for the Landscape Architecture Foundation (Francis 1999a, 2000a). The method was developed to provide a uniform and comparable way to document and evaluate landscape architecture projects and issues. In this earlier work, I suggested that LAF commission three types of case studies in landscape architecture: place-based, issue-based, and hypothetical case studies for teaching. This is the first issue-based case study for LAF with several others to follow. It is intended as a prototype or template for others to adopt or modify.

The case study method for specific landscapes involves the collection and analysis of different kinds of information including archival research, examination of the role of key project participants, financial aspects, project goals, and the design and decision making process. In addition, site-specific case studies document use, perceptions, unique constraints, project successes, and limitations.

In contrast to place-specific case studies of a single park or plaza, issue-based case studies look across several cases to define common patterns and themes. They also look across places and previous case studies to identify design or management principles that can guide future practice. Table 2 provides a suggested format for issue-based case studies.

This issue-based case study looks across several past studies to glean significant findings and design implications related to designing for user needs in urban open spaces. This case study is based on interviews with practitioners and researchers on what they consider to be the most important issues and advances in open space design and planning, identification of best practices, and suggestions of future research and design issues.

OPPOSITE Active engagement in the environment, such as these boys biking in a Paris square, is an ingredient of a successful urban open space.

TABLE 2

A SUGGESTED FORMAT FOR ISSUE-BASED CASE STUDIES

ABSTRACT/FACT SHEET
Issue Name
Landscape Type
Issue Significance and Impact
Lessons Learned
Contacts
Keywords

FULL CASE STUDY
Issue Background and History
Genesis of Issue
Past Research/Case Studies on Issue
Design, Development, and Decision Making Implications
Role of Landscape Architect(s)
Maintenance and Management Approaches
User/Use Analysis
Peer Reviews of Issue
Criticism
Significance and Uniqueness of Issue
Limitations/Problems
Generalizable Features and Lessons
Future Issues/Plans
Implications/Recommendations
Conclusions/Directions for Future Work
Contacts for Further Information
Bibliography
Useful Web Sites/Listservs
Useful Journals

GRAPHICS
Photograph(s) of Issue and Past Case Studies
Site Plan(s) to Scale of Case Study Sites

This case study was developed using the following methods:

- Archival research on user needs and conflicts in urban open space
- Published case studies of urban open spaces
- Internet searches
- Selected site visits to urban open spaces to observe open space use and conflicts
- Interviews with key experts
- Interviews with open space designers and managers
- Interviews with open space users

CASE STUDY IN LAND & COMMUNITY DESIGN

ISSUE NAME

Urban Open Space, Designing for User Needs

LANDSCAPE TYPE

Urban open spaces, including parks, plazas, streets, gardens, and others

SIGNIFICANCE & IMPACT

Needs and conflicts affect how open spaces are used experienced, and valued

LESSONS LEARNED

Careful attention to user needs can create more successful open spaces

CONTACTS

Urban Parks Institute

Trust for Public Land

American Society of Landscape Architects

Landscape Architecture Foundation

Environmental Design Research Association

Project for Public Spaces

Local and State Parks Departments

Open Space Districts

KEYWORDS

open space, parks, plazas, waterfronts, needs, comfort, relaxation, passive engagement, active engagement, discovery, conflicts, user groups, design, planning, management

URBAN OPEN SPACES
WHY SOME WORK AND OTHERS DON'T

Providing for human use and enjoyment is a basic requirement in creating and maintaining successful open spaces. Past studies of parks, plazas, and neighborhood open spaces definitively have shown that providing for human needs is a prerequisite for successful public spaces. Yet too many spaces still suffer from lack of attention to user needs. As a result, conflicts occur that limit open space use and create expensive and ongoing management and maintenance problems.

Many open spaces work well but others are empty, unsafe, or dysfunctional. What makes a successful public space? This can be determined in part by looking at places that do not respond to human needs and are not used. They are often empty of people or, if used, have significant conflicts between different user groups or between users and management. The Project for Public Spaces, a non-profit organization that carries on the work of its founder, William H. Whyte, has evaluated hundreds of spaces in North America and abroad and has developed a systematic process to program and design spaces (PPS 2000). Several of the Project for Public Spaces findings for why spaces fail are included in Table 3.

There are several conditions that limit human use and enjoyment in public open spaces. Perhaps the most dominant barrier is an over emphasis on art and aesthetics. Spaces sometimes are designed to be viewed as abstract art forms with few human amenities. This design culture is reinforced by journals and design award programs that promote design excellence with photographs of landscapes without people. Such aesthetics-only designs have become more limited as public and private clients insist that spaces be designed for people first, rather than art. In addition, concerns of security, fear of undesirables, and unrealistic construction budgets sometimes limit the design of open spaces for user needs.

OPPOSITE Many New York City plazas were moved indoors and privatized.

The Project for Public Spaces (PPS) suggests four main ingredients that make great public open spaces: accessibility, activities, comfort and sociability (PPS 2000: 18–19). According to PPS (2000: 17), *accessibility* includes such factors as linkages, walkability, connectedness and convenience that can be measured through behavior mapping of use, pedestrian activity and traffic data. *Activities* include uses, celebration, usefulness, and sustainability and are measured by property values, changes in land use, and retail sales. *Comfort* includes elements such as safety, good places to sit, attractiveness, and cleanliness. These can be measured through crime statistics, building conditions, and environmental data. *Sociability* involves dimensions such as friendliness, interactivity, and diversity and can be assessed by studies of street use, diversity of users, and social networks. Table 4 outlines the principles PPS proposes to create great public open spaces.

TABLE 3

WHY PUBLIC SPACES FAIL

- Lack of good places to sit
- Lack of gathering points
- Poor entrances and visually inaccessible spaces
- Dysfunctional features
- Paths that don't go where people want to go
- Domination of a place by vehicles
- Blank walls or dead zones around the edges of a place
- Inconveniently located transit stops
- Nothing going on

Source: Project for Public Spaces, *How to Turn a Place Around,* 2000: 21–29.

TABLE 4
_____

PRINCIPLES OF CREATING GREAT PUBLIC SPACES

UNDERLYING IDEAS

1. The community is the expert
2. You are creating the place—not a design
3. You can't do it alone
4. They always say it can't be done

PLANNING AND OUTREACH TECHNIQUES

5. You can see a lot by just observing
6. Develop a vision

TRANSLATING IDEAS INTO ACTION

7. Form supports function
8. Triangulate

IMPLEMENTATION

9. Start with petunias
10. Money is not the issue
11. You are never finished

Source: Project for Public Spaces, *How to Turn a Place Around,* 2000: 33.

How do we know when a place works for people? PPS suggests five indicators of a highly successful public open space (PPS 2000: 81–83). First, a high proportion of people in groups use space. Second, a higher than average proportion of women use the space, which indicates a higher level of perceived safety and comfort. Third, different age groups use the space, together and at different times of the day. Fourth, a range of varied activities occur simultaneously. Fifth, more activities of affection are present, such as smiling, kissing, embracing, and holding hands.

Addressing user needs has been identified in numerous studies as a basic requirement in creating and maintaining successful open spaces. Past studies of parks, plazas, and neighborhood open spaces have shown conclusively that adequately providing for user needs is a prerequisite to good public spaces.

A children's garden, Brooklyn, New York.

Downtown pedestrian walkway,
Los Angeles, California.

Las Ramblas, Barcelona, Spain.

THE RESEARCH ON
URBAN PARKS AND OPEN SPACE

User needs have been identified in a wide variety of case studies as an important ingredient for successful urban parks and open spaces. Awareness of people's needs first came into the forefront as the result of the pioneering work of William H. Whyte (1980, 1988) through his observations of the use and nonuse of plazas in New York City. User needs have since been identified by organizations such as the Urban Parks Institute (UPI), Project for Public Spaces (PPS), and Trust for Public Land (TPL) as one of the most critical considerations in planning, designing and managing urban parks and open spaces.[2]

Concern for user needs has increased due to the growing public support for open space preservation and development (TPL 1994). Voters across the country have been consistently approving major bond measures for open space ranging from purchase of sensitive open lands to development of urban parks and gardens. For example, in 2000, California voters passed a multi-billion dollar park and open space initiative, and the state legislature and governor have provided $75 million in matching money to purchase sensitive habitats and open spaces.

This pattern has been repeated in states and cities across the country. The American Society of Landscape Architects (ASLA) reports that in the November 2000 election, twenty-five states approved more than seventy-five measures committing a total of three billion dollars or the preservation of open space and the enhancement of recreation opportunities.[3] Most of these projects will require attention to user needs to be successful.

---

2 / Other key factors include programming, financing, management, and maintenance. See Harnik 2000, and Garvin and Berens 1997, for recent surveys of urban parks and the factors that influence their success.

3 / See Marcia Argust, "Today's Political Landscape, LAND," *ASLA*.

Passive engagement, including finding a quiet place to sleep, is an ingredient of a successful public space. Lafayette Park, Washington, DC.

Awareness of the importance of considering people in open space design also results from public policy efforts to create new public open spaces. Notable examples are zoning requirements, in effect in New York City since the early 1960s, that established new public plazas and parks. City planners have provided developers with bonuses of increased building height and bulk for providing new public open spaces, and these policies have resulted in hundreds of new plazas in the city. Yet there have been concerns expressed about the "publicness" of these spaces (Madden and Love 1982; The Parks Council 1993).

A study by Harvard urban design professor Jerold S. Kayden (2000) shows that there are significant problems with many of these spaces in New York City. Kayden states: "At their worst, by design and operation, the spaces have been hostile to public use. Brasseries bulge, cafes creep and trattorias trickle into adjacent public space, confusing users who think that they must pay the price of a meal or drink to sit at a table and enjoy the space" (2000: 75). Concerns such as these have led some cities to reassess their open space policies and design guidelines.

TABLE 5

CASE STUDIES OF USER NEEDS IN OPEN SPACE

ISSUE-BASED CASE STUDIES

Children (Hart 1978; Moore 1986; Goltsman et al. 1987; Holloway and Valentine 2000)

Control (Carr and Lynch 1981; Francis 1989a)

Defensible Space (Newman 1973)

Economic Benefits (TPL 1994)

Environmental Education (Moore and Wong 1997)

History (Cranz 1982; Tishler 1989)

Homelessness (Bunston and Breton 1992)

Participation (Hester 1990, 1999; Hart 1997; Francis 1999b)

Sunlight in Public Spaces (Bosselmann 1983)

Teenagers (Owens 1998)

Urban Space (Hiss 1990)

Vegetation (Ulrich 1981, 1984; Moore 1993)

Women in Public Space (Franck and Paxson 1989).

PLACE-BASED CASE STUDIES

Bryant Park, New York City (Berens 1998; Thompson 1997; Francis 2000a)

Central Park, New York City (Barlow 1987; Lindsay 1977; Beveridge et al. 1995)

Central Park and Davis Farmers Market, Davis, California (Carr et al. 1992; Francis 1999c)

City Hall Plaza, Boston, Massachusetts (Carr et al. 1992)

Gas Works Park, Seattle, Washington (Hester 1983)

Grand Street Waterfront Park, Brooklyn, New York (Francis et al. 1984)

Lovejoy and Forecourt Fountain, Portland, Oregon (Love 1973)

Manteo, North Carolina (Hester 1985)

Pershing Park, Washington, DC (Carr et al. 1992)

Pompidou Centre, Paris (Carr et al. 1992)

Plaza Park, Sacramento, California (Sommer and Becker 1969)

Seagrams Plaza, New York City (Whyte 1980)

Steps of the New York Public Library, New York City (Carr et al. 1992)

Urban Wildlife Preserve, Sacramento, California (Francis and Bowns 2001)

Village Homes, Davis, California (Francis 2001)

CASE STUDIES OF TYPES OF OPEN SPACE

Adventure Playgrounds (Cooper 1970)

Children's Environments (Hart 1978; Moore 1986; Goltsman et al. 1987)

Community Gardens and Open Spaces (Fox et al. 1985; Francis et al. 1984; Warner 1987)

Healing Gardens (Cooper Marcus and Barnes 1999; Bedard 2000)

Markets (Seamon and Nordon 1980; Sommer 1989)

Plazas (Whyte 1980, 1988; Gehl and Gemoze 1996)

Streets (Brower 1988; Vernez-Moudon 1987; Jacobs 1961; Gehl and Gemoze 1996)

Sustainable Neighborhoods (Francis 2001)

Urban Parks (Cochran et al. 1998; Harnik 2000)

Urban Wilds (Hester et al. 2000)

Past case studies and research on user needs and conflicts have ranged from site-specific case studies of parks and open spaces, to research that examines specific issues or user groups. These include studies on the needs of children (Hart 1978; Moore 1986; Goltsman et al. 1987) and teenagers (Owens 1998); defensible space (Newman 1973); economic benefits (TPL 1994); and the role of sunlight in parks and plazas (Bosselmann 1983). A list of some of these past studies is included in Table 5.

User Needs

Past studies have addressed user needs in specific types of open spaces, as shown in Table 5 on page 19. A content analysis of these and other past studies of open space reveal at least five major categories of needs that should be considered in the design and management of public space. These needs include comfort, relaxation, passive engagement, active engagement, and discovery. In addition, this case study adds a sixth—fun—as it has largely been ignored in previous studies of outdoor spaces. While past studies show that user needs may differ somewhat by age (for example between children, teenagers, adults, and the elderly), sex, and cultural differences, these user needs are common to most people's enjoyment of open space. Each is summarized in the pages following.

Comfort

For an open space to be well used, it needs to be comfortable (Carr et al. 1992). This may simply mean providing enough comfortable places to sit or management practices that invite use. The need for food, drink, shelter from the elements, or a place to rest when tired requires some degree of comfort to be satisfied. Without comfort it is difficult for other needs to be met, although people sometimes will endure major discomforts in attempts to enjoy themselves. In addition, relief from sun or access to

A good public place provides comfortable seating.

Pioneer Square in Portland is designed as a comfortable plaza.

Providing for relaxation makes Paley Park in New York City an inviting space.

There are many different ways to provide for relaxation, as on Church Street in Burlington, Vermont.

Gardening is one way to provide for active engagement in public space.

School and community gardens provide opportunities for active engagement.

sun is a major factor in the use of open spaces (Bosselmann 1983; Whyte 1980). The various forms of accessibility, including physical and symbolic access, are also basic prerequisites to comfort. This also includes the special needs of children and the elderly as well as needs addressed by the guidelines of the Americans with Disabilities Act (ADA) and the Consumer Product Safety Commission.

Relaxation

Research on open spaces indicates that people frequently seek outdoor settings for relaxation. A sense of psychological comfort is one of the experiences people look for in open spaces. This benefit can be provided by the restorative effects of water or vegetation, including the psychological effects of plants (Cooper Marcus and Barnes 1999; Lewis 1996; Ulrich and Addoms 1981). It may also result in specific health and physiological effects such as reduction of stress or decreased blood pressure (Ulrich 1981, 1984). Considerable empirical research has shown that the healing power of landscapes often results from perceived or real relaxation (Bedard 2000; Taylor, Kuo, and Sullivan 2001; Cooper Marcus and Barnes 1999).[4]

Passive Engagement

Passive engagement is the way most people experience open spaces. It can lead to a sense of relaxation but it differs in that it involves the need for an encounter with the setting without becoming actively involved (Carr et al. 1992). This includes the enjoyment people derive from watching the passing scene. It may be indirect or passive, such as looking rather than talking or doing. Passive activities include sitting, reading, people watching, day dreaming, sleeping or simply tuning out things around you. Performers or programmed activities often help facilitate this kind of activity (PPS 2000). Observing games and sporting events offers a kind of passive engagement as well.

Active Engagement

This need frequently involves some physical involvement with the space. Open space has a long tradition of satisfying this need by providing for various types of

---

4 / Together this work provides empirical evidence that designed and natural landscapes have important health and psychological benefits. While landscape architects have argued this since Olmsted, only in the last decades has solid empirical research proven this conclusively.

LEFT Park Guell in Barcelona provides opportunities for discovery.

RIGHT The Infant Garden at a preschool in Davis, California, designed by landscape architect Susan Herrington, provides opportunities for movement and discovery.

OPPOSITE Nature provides children with important opportunities for discovery.

sports or physical activities (Cranz 1982). Other forms of active engagement with the environment include walking and gardening. This need has given rise to newer and popular forms of open spaces such as community gardens (Warner 1987; Francis et al. 1984) and greenways (Flink and Stearns 1993; Schwartz et al. 1993). The new types of spaces have been found to satisfy user needs not afforded in more traditional types of open spaces (Francis 1989b). For example, in an earlier study of a community garden in Sacramento, the author found that while park users make use of diverse types of parks, community gardeners typically do not use parks (Francis 1987c). Community gardening is a form of active engagement that continues over time in order to sustain and preserve the garden (Fox et al. 1985).

Discovery

Discovery can take many forms ranging from viewing public art and sculpture to stumbling upon unexpected places. Open spaces can also provide important opportunities for discovery-based learning and education (Stine 1997; Adams 1990; Johnson 2000). The development of natural areas (Francis and Bowns 2001); school yards (Moore and Wong 1997); and school gardens (Moore 1986, 1993) are some examples of increased awareness that landscape can be used to promote learning.[5]

Fun

An important and often overlooked user need is the desire for fun or excitement in public spaces. Theme and amusement park developers such as the Disney Corporation understand this need and charge good money to experience it, although often in a private, highly-controlled environment. While much of the popularity of theme parks falls into the previous categories of comfort, relaxation, and passive engagement, fun and its various dimensions, such as mystery, adventure, and challenge, is an important ingredient of good open spaces. Examples of public open

---

5 / One of the most developed and impressive examples of this is the "Learning Through Landscapes Initiative" in Britain. See Adams 1990.

spaces that address these needs include adventure playgrounds (Cooper 1970; Nicholson 1971) and skateboard parks (Jones and Graves 2000).

User Conflicts

User conflicts are often common in urban open spaces. They may result from a lack of attention to user needs, poor design, or larger social problems such as drug use or homelessness. Some conflict, such as diverse groups competing for open space, is healthy as it creates a necessary tension between freedom and control (Carr and Lynch 1981; Francis 1989a). Yet good programming, design, and management can help to avoid many user conflicts.

Past studies have found that user conflicts often result from lack of concern for context (Chidister 1986; Joardar and Neill 1978); economic factors (Fox 1990; Colorado State Trails Program 1995); equity differences (Jones forthcoming); lack of public access (Lynch 1972); and privatization (Kayden 2000). A number of books examine user conflicts: *People Places* (Cooper Marcus and Francis 1998); *Yard, Street, Park* (Girling and Helphand 1994); *Life Between Buildings* (Gehl 1987); and *Public Space* (Carr et al. 1992). Others have examined historical, theoretical, or sociological aspects of user conflicts in open spaces. Important examples include *The Experience of Place* (Hiss 1990); *The Language of Landscape* (Spirn 1999); *The Death and Life of Great American Cities* (Jacobs 1961); *The Politics of Park Design* (Cranz 1982); *City as Landscape* (Turner 1996); and *The Experience of Nature* (Kaplan and Kaplan 1999). Two recent national studies of parks and open spaces prepared by the Trust for Public Land and the Urban Land Institute, *Inside City Parks* (Harnik 2000) and *Urban Parks and Open Spaces* (Garvin and Berens 1997), identify common conflicts that exist in urban parks nationally.

These past case studies have identified several types of conflicts ranging from conflicts between different types of users (such as teenagers and the elderly), to more complicated cultural differences (for example between different ethnic and economic groups). I will briefly discuss a few of the most common varieties.

Safety/Security

A condition of one's enjoyment of open space is perceived safety and security. Fear of crime and violence, especially against women, can cause seemingly good spaces to go unused (Franck and Paxson 1989). While there is often a difference between

Challenge and risk are ingredients of fun.

The Sail Boat Pond, Central Park, New York City.

Historical analysis is one useful way to address issues of user needs and conflicts.

actual and perceived crime and danger in public open spaces, fear often leads to people avoiding spaces—even well-designed and attractive ones.

Abuse

Most conflicts over open space result from abuse of places (Gold 1972). Typical examples of abuse in urban parks include vandalism and dominance by one user group over others. City parks departments and open space managers often experience increased costs due to the abuse of spaces. Design and programming have been found to be the most effective ways to successfully avoid abuse of urban open spaces (Cooper Marcus and Francis 1998; Carr et al. 1992).

Conflicts Between User Groups

Conflicts between different types of user groups are common and difficult to manage. Examples include conflicts between hikers and mountain bikers in urban parks, dog owners and other park users, children and traffic (Sandels 1975), and skateboarders and plaza users (Jones and Graves 2000). Conflicts may result from so-called "undesirables" and homeless people (Sommer and Becker 1969; Rivlin 1996; Mitchell 1998). These conflicts can often be effectively addressed through good programming, design, or management. For example, increasing the density and diversity of users has been found to be one of the best ways to reduce conflicts and increase public space use and enjoyment (Francis 1999c).

Direct control is an important part of successful public space.

Cultural Differences

Some observers of open space suggest that conflicts in open space result from cultural and class differences (Arreola 1995; Hester 1975; Lindsay 1977; Loukaitou-Sideris 1995). Some of these conflicts result from the way different groups use open space. UCLA planner Loukaitou-Sideris (1995) found that Hispanic and African Americans in Los Angeles are more likely to use parks for stationary activities such as social gathering and hanging out (passive engagement). There are signs that this may be changing. As more and more

Skateparks such as the Burnside Park in Portland, Oregon, are a good way to design teenagers into public open spaces.

Skateboarders are often discouraged from public open spaces due to their conflicts with other users. Freedom Plaza, Washington, DC.

Many public open spaces are used differently than they were intended, such as this plaza in Kobe, Japan.

Some spaces are designed for viewing only, such as this space in Sausalito, California, with a sign that reads: "This historical park is for your viewing pleasure only."

Americans are becoming comfortable hanging out in open spaces, cultural disparities between different user groups may decline.[6] Hanging out is clearly becoming a more common form of open space use.

In a recent study of the wilderness areas in and around Los Angeles, Randy Hester and his colleagues examine the real and perceived conflicts that exist between cultural groups as a means of showing how different groups use urban open space (Hester et al. 2000). They summarize and then discount several common myths about users and their connection to wilderness areas. They found, contrary to common belief, that "people of color appreciate the benefits of urban wilderness and are one of the groups most supportive of open space land acquisition and park development" (Hester et al. 2000: 137). Furthermore, they determine that the use of urban wilds by minorities and ethnic groups is not harmful to habitat preservation and creation. They conclude that future planning and design of urban parks "hinge on the integration of biological and social concerns" (Hester et al. 2000: 137).

Gender Conflicts

There has been increased understanding that women often have more specialized needs in open spaces than men (Franck and Paxson 1989; Mozingo 1989; Bunston and Breton 1992). Women have been found to feel less comfortable using some public spaces, especially if they seem uninviting or unsafe. The needs of safety, security, and comfort are especially important to consider in the design of urban space for women.

---

6 / One of the benefits of Starbucks and the growing café culture in cities is that Americans are once again becoming comfortable hanging out in public places. Past studies have documented the historic hanging about in places such as taverns and bars, on street corners, in candy stores, and in bookstores; this activity has decreased over time. The author remembers a discussion years ago with the Danish urban designer Jan Gehl, who argued that Americans could never be walkers and sitters like Danes. The author hopes we are proving him wrong on both points.

Many public spaces are designed to discourage homeless people.

People of all abilities need to be considered in design, as in the case of the Central Park Children's Fountain in Davis, California.

Ability

There are increased requirements for equal access to open spaces for people of all abilities. The impact of legislation such as the Americans with Disabilities Act (ADA) is that designers create places that meet minimum code requirements without actually meeting the needs of the users that the laws were put in place to support. The result is that some designers are practicing segregation rather than inclusion in the design of public space (Jones and Welch 1999).

Privatization of Public Space

A continuing conflict exists over privatization versus publicness in open spaces (The Parks Council 1993; Kayden 2000). With decreased public support for developing and managing parks, plazas, and playgrounds, the private sector has become a major funder and developer of open spaces. With the increased involvement of developers and building owners in park development has come increased concern over the degree of control they exert over what was historically publicly owned and managed spaces. Private-public partnerships are now common in developing or redeveloping urban open spaces. Yet these are often controversial and create concerns about whether these spaces belong to adjacent building owners or the public. Virtually every city has examples of public debates over the privatization of open spaces. Notable examples include the current redesigns proposed for Boston's City Hall Plaza, New York's Bryant Park, and San Francisco's Union Square.

Conflicts Between Use and Ecology

A growing concern in open spaces is the perceived conflict between human use and ecology. Ecologists and natural scientists frequently argue that people and wildlife need to be separated and protected from one another. This is also true in urban parks such as New York City's Prospect Park, where the Prospect Park Alliance has fenced off a section of the woodland area to restore it to its Olmstedian glories. There is some concern over the huge cost of this effort and lack of attention to other areas.

Sea Ranch, in Northern California, was designed to balance both human and ecological needs.

While there is solid scientific support for protected habitat, there is also a growing conflict between the public's desire for increased access to nearby nature and ecologists' plans to create habitat separate from people. As environmental concerns expand along with people's desire for access to more natural, undeveloped open space, this conflict will surely increase. Yet there are some useful and encouraging studies that show that natural areas can be used by people without significantly damaging habitat (Gobster and Hull 2000; Kaplan et al. 1998; Hough 1995). This has been shown to be also true with people of diverse backgrounds and open-space needs (Hester et al. 2000).

DESIGN, DEVELOPMENT, AND DECISION-MAKING

Virtually all of these past studies point to the importance of good design and management in making successful public spaces. Several case studies have produced a number of concepts useful for incorporating user needs into the design or redesign of open space. Examples include studies and redesigns of Bryant Park (Berens 1998; Thompson 1997; Nager and Wentworth 1977; Francis 2000a), Seagrams Plaza (Whyte 1980), the steps of the New York Public Library (Carr et al. 1992) and Central Park in New York City (Barlow 1987; Lindsay 1977; Beveridge et al. 1995). In addition, case studies of City Hall Plaza in Boston (Carr et al. 1992); Gas Works Park in Seattle (Hester 1983; Carr et al. 1992); Lovejoy and Forecourt Fountain in Portland, Oregon (Love 1973); Manteo, North Carolina (Hester 1985); the Pompidou Centre in Paris (Carr et al. 1992); Plaza Park in Sacramento (Sommer and Becker 1969); and Central Park and Davis Farmers Market in Davis, California (Francis 1999c) have all produced useful design principles based on user needs.

Some socially-minded designers and researchers have translated user needs into suggested designs and design guidelines for urban open spaces.[7] William H. Whyte, widely recognized as the pioneer in analyzing the social uses of urban open spaces, has provided a set of useful guidelines for designing urban public space (Whyte 1980, 1998). He found that adequate sitting space ("people sit where there are places to sit"), food, access to the sun, protection from wind, and the provision of water and vegetation are all essential ingredients for a space to be well used (Whyte 1980). He was also an early advocate for incorporating the street into the design of urban public space, arguing against creating separate spaces from the street's public environment. Whyte wrote guidelines for new public open spaces, which were adopted in large part by the City of New York in the creation of new open space. A *NOVA* public television program he produced about his work in the early 1980s brought awareness of these concerns to a larger audience; a tape of the program is frequently used to train design students in Whyte's unique way of looking at public spaces. The Project for Public Spaces in New York City carries on his work and many of his ideas have become standard practice and policy.

Landscape architects such as Lawrence Halprin and Randy Hester, and more recently Walter Hood and Laurie Olin (see Bryant Park Case Study), have demonstrated in their projects that successful open spaces are a function of successful design. Halprin (1970; 1998) has shown in much of his work, such as the Portland Lovejoy and Forecourt Fountains, and the FDR Memorial in Washington, DC, that design can be used to address user complexity, choreography of use, and human dynamics. Laurie Olin, in an impressive number of new parks and public spaces in San Francisco, New York City, and elsewhere, has shown that good design and user needs can be successfully combined.

Farmers markets enliven urban open spaces.

---

7 / Notable examples include Walter Hood, *Urban Diaries* (1997); Diane Karasov, *The Once and Future Park* (1993); Kevin Lynch, *Good City Form* (1981); and Peter Rowe, *Civic Realism* (1997). There are several useful design guidelines for urban open spaces, including Cooper Marcus et al., *People Places* (1998); Jan Gehl, *Life Between Buildings* (1987); and Girling et al., *Yard, Street, Park* (1994).

Programmed activities, such as this performance in a Parisan square, enhance the use of a public space.

Trails and greenways for walking and running are receiving increased use, such as this public trail at The Sea Ranch in Northern California.

There is an expanding variety of open space types such as children's gardens like this one in Brooklyn, New York.

Study after study has shown that design alone is not enough to create successful public spaces. Too many examples exist of seemingly well-designed spaces that ignore basic principles of user needs. Addressing user needs is a critical factor in effective design and should be considered in the design of any space, no matter how large or small. If spaces ignore human needs, then they are not well designed.

While designing for user needs may differ by open space types or context, some basic principles are common to most types of open space.

• Design and management should address user needs for any open space.

• Programming is critical to addressing user needs.

• People's rights for access, appropriation, and use must be protected in the design and management of open spaces.

• Users and even some nonusers (such as adjacent residents) should be directly involved in the design and management of open spaces (Hester 1990, Kretzman et al. 1993).

• User and stakeholder participation should be real, not token (Hart 1997; Hester 1999).

• Design and management should incorporate the visions of the designer(s) and users (Hester 1999, Francis 1999b).

• Adaptability and flexibility should be designed into projects (Gehl and Gemoze 1996).

• Ongoing evaluation and redesign are critical to the life of any open space (Cooper Marcus et al. 1998).

The Park now has a constituency of tens of thousands of people. It's going to endure.

—Laurie Olin, 1997

BRYANT PARK
A CASE STUDY OF DESIGNING FOR USER NEEDS

The history of Bryant Park graphically demonstrates some of the conflicts inherent in managing public spaces in dense urban centers. Considering its location in the center of New York City, the notion of Bryant Park as a place for relaxation can be viewed as appropriate on one hand and unrealistic on the other. Clearly many urbanites seek a place of retreat from the activity of the city, and Bryant Park is one of the few places in central Manhattan that could conceivably offer this respite. Indeed, in their 1976 study of the park, Nager and Wentworth found that relaxing or resting was the most frequent activity engaged in by the people they interviewed in the park.

However, as Nager and Wentworth suggest, some of the very factors that made Bryant Park a place for retreat and relaxation—such as its ample vegetation and the stone fences separating it from the street—also made it a popular place for drug dealers, who operated easily in the semi-seclusion of the park from the 1970s until its redevelopment in the 1990s.[8] During the 1970s it became clear that some design or management changes were necessary in order to counteract the appropriation of the park by dealers and their clients and to increase its use by a wider range of people, including local office workers and shoppers. This concern gave rise to Bryant Park's redesign and development, completed between 1991 and 1995.

OPPOSITE Bryant Park after redesign in the 1990s.

---

8 / Material for this case is drawn from Biederman and Nager, "Up from Smoke: A New Improved Bryant Park?" (1981); Carr et al., *Public Space* (1992); Garvin and Berens, *Urban Parks and Open Space* (1997); Longo, *Great American Public Places* (1996); Nager and Wentworth, "Bryant Park: A Comprehensive Evaluation of Its Image and Use with Implications for Urban Open Space Design" (1976); and Thompson, *The Rebirth of New York City's Bryant Park* (1997).

PROJECT NAME	BRYANT PARK, NEW YORK, NEW YORK
LOCATION	Avenue of the Americas, between 41st and 42nd Streets, behind New York Public Library
DATE DESIGNED/PLANNED	Original design completed in 1934; redesigned early 1990s
CONSTRUCTION COMPLETED	Built in phases from 1991 to 1995
CONSTRUCTION COST	$5.9 million for park rehabilitation
SIZE	4.6 acres
LANDSCAPE ARCHITECTS	Hanna/Olin, Landscape Architects
CLIENT/DEVELOPER	New York City Parks Department and Bryant Park Restoration Corporation (BPRC)
CONSULTANT/ARCHITECT	Hardy Holzman Pfeiffer, New York City
MANAGED BY	New York City Parks Department and Bryant Park Restoration Corporation (BPRC)

Bryant Park before redesign was a popular place for drug dealers.

Context

Bryant Park, located one block east of Times Square and immediately behind the main branch of the New York Public Library, is a large public open space in Manhattan's congested midtown. It is located in a dense office and educational district and serves as an outdoor retreat for office workers, visitors, and students. While it was heavily used by drug dealers and homeless people in the 1970s, today it is heralded as a revitalized and democratic urban public space that serves as a model for other cities.

Site Analysis

Bryant Park is bounded on three sides by streets and on the fourth by the rear façade of the New York Public Library. Two of the three streets, 42nd Street and Avenue of the Americas, are heavily trafficked. Historic elements include a stand of heritage sycamore trees on the site framing a central lawn area and a plaza at the western end. There are stunning views of the skyline of midtown Manhattan from most parts of the park, and the New York Public Library building, designed by eminent architects Carrère & Hastings, forms a strong visual edge at the east end of the park. Anita Nager and Wally Wentworth (1976) conducted a behavioral analysis of Bryant Park in the early 1970s, followed by filming and observation of use of the park by the sociologist William Whyte (1979). Landscape architect Laurie Olin completed detailed sketches, site analyses, and redesign studies of the park in 1980s.[9] Several economic studies evaluated the importance and redevelopment of the park during that same period.

---

9 / See Olin's engaging sketches, in W. Thompson, *The Rebirth of New York City's Bryant Park* (1997), 9–17.

Project Background and History

While Bryant Park has served as a public open space since the mid-1850s, its main configuration was established in 1934, and then modified in the early 1990s. Bryant Park was originally a potter's field in 1823. It was developed as a park in 1847, and named Reservoir Park, "after the city reservoir that was constructed on the site now occupied by the public library" (Berens 1998: 45). In 1884 it was renamed Bryant Park after the poet William Cullen Bryant, who was a strong advocate of parks. When Robert Moses became head of the New York City Parks Department in 1923, he mounted a major redevelopment of the park. Moses intended it to be a place of "restful beauty," with ample trees and hedges, rather than a space for active recreation (Biederman and Nager 1981). Moses held a design competition and the winning design converted the park into a classically-influenced formal space surrounded by a stone fence, laid out in a symmetrical fashion.

Bryant Park was designed originally in an open, classical style.

Before the Moses redesign, the park land was on the same grade as the surrounding sidewalks. With the Moses park design, ground fill from nearby subway construction raised the park above street level. Gayle Berens of the Urban Land Institute (ULI), who has written an excellent and detailed case study of the park, attributes the decline of the park to the late 1960s when it was "ignored by leisure-time" users (Berens 1998: 46). The recent 1990s redevelopment largely addressed the perception of Bryant Park as a "needle park" for drug dealing (Longo 1996). Years of neglect, deterioration, and problems of use led the Rockefeller Brothers Fund to finance a reexamination of the park. The fund brought in William Whyte, who used his extensive research on the park to create a formula for redesign.

After Whyte's report, the Bryant Park Restoration Corporation (BPRC), a public-private partnership, was formed to redevelop the park, and a team of designers was hired. Construction of the park took place in the early 1990s and it has enjoyed a rebirth as a result. Today it is a well-used and popular open space in midtown Manhattan.

Genesis of the Project

The Bryant Park redevelopment grew out of significant social and crime problems with the park. To redevelop the park, the Rockefeller Brothers Fund and private corporations located near the park founded the BPRC in 1980. While the corporation dealt extensively with maintenance and security issues in cooperation with the city's parks and police departments, its major goal was "to fill Bryant Park with activity, to attract to the park as many legitimate users as possible" (BPRC 1981). In the years it has operated, the restoration group, in conjunction with the Parks Council, the Public Art Fund, and other organizations, has been responsible for an array of events and new activities in the park. These include several concert series, an artists-in-residence program, arts-and-crafts shows, a booth selling half-price tickets to musical and dance events, and book and flower stalls (Carr et al. 1992). It is generally agreed that these activities, along with improvements in policing and maintenance, significantly increased park use and reduced crime (Cranz 1982). However, it was clear that more had to be done to restore and refresh the park. BPRC hired landscape architects Hanna/Olin in the early 1990s to redesign the park. The firm's design goal was to make the park a multi-use and user-friendly urban open space.

Bryant Park in the 1970s and 1980s was a popular "people" place during weekday lunchtime but underused at other times.

Design and Development Process

Approximately $5 million worth of physical changes were made to the park in several phases in the early 1990s: adding more seating; increasing access points; refurbishing hedges, lawns, and flower beds; restoring the fountains and the Bryant statue; and expanding the library's central book stacks underneath the Great Lawn. The architectural office of Hardy Holzman Pfeiffer Associates was hired to design the historically compatible restaurant addition at the rear of the New York Public Library, which faces the park. The proposal to build the restaurant, viewed as an encroachment into the public park with a private development, caused considerable opposition, including objections from the influential private advocacy group, the Parks Council. After three years of public debate and review, a scaled-down plan called for two smaller buildings, one housing an upscale restaurant and the other for small concessions selling lower-cost food. The redesign, a heavily scheduled events program, increased maintenance (including an annual budget of $2 million and 35 full-time staff), and such new elements as food, music, and movable seating have provided the ultimate formula for success (Thompson 1997; Berens 1998).

Role of the Landscape Architect

Landscape architect Laurie Olin and his firm Hanna/Olin played a major role in the design and redevelopment of Bryant Park. Their concern was "design, rather than sociology," since the existing park had many physical problems ranging from years of neglect to numerous dead ends, hidden places, and a general lack of amenities. In the end, many of the changes were subtle, building on the classical principles of Moses's 1930s design.

Program Elements

The park redesign program was essentially identified in the original behavioral research done by Anita Nager and Wally Wentworth, two doctoral students in environmental psychology at the City University Graduate Center, which directly faces the park (Nager and Wentworth 1976). William Whyte summed up the park's problems by stating that "access is the nub of the matter. Psychologically, as well as physically, Bryant Park is a hidden place. The best way to meet the problem is to promote the widest possible use and enjoyment by people" (Berens 1998: 46). Whyte translated this observation into a number of specific recommendations in 1979:

- Remove the iron fences.
- Remove the shrubbery.
- Cut openings in the balustrades for easier pedestrian circulation in and out of the park.
- Improve visual access up the steps on the Avenue of the Americas.
- Provide a third set of steps midway between the existing stairs and 42nd Street.
- Provide ramps for the handicapped.
- Open up access to the terrace at the back of the library with new steps.
- Restore the fountain.
- Rehabilitate Carrère and Hastings' historic restroom structures.

While all these ideas were not adopted in the final design program, they became the essential redesign agenda for Bryant Park. A number of additional elements were included in the park, such as 2,000 movable folding chairs and extensive new planting to make the edge of the park more like a public garden. The restrooms were also restored, complete with fresh flowers and a baby-changing table.

Bryant Park has become a major outdoor space in New York City, heavily used since the 1990s redesign.

Maintenance and Management

One of the keys to the park's rebirth (as described in recent case studies of Bryant Park) was its extensive management and maintenance program (Berens 1998; Thompson 1997). Aggressive events programming has clearly played a key in the park's success. For example, Bryant Park and the BPRC have hosted several free concerts, high-profile fashion shows, and public fairs on a regular basis. A staff of 35 maintains and manages the park, including "a full-time horticulturist, a maintenance and sanitation crew, and a security team that operates 24 hours a day, seven days a week" (Thompson 1997: 33). This unusually high level of maintenance is made possible by a unique public-private partnership between the city of New York (which in many ways gave up its claim to maintaining the park), corporate and institutional tenants of surrounding buildings, and the private foundations. A Business Improvement District (BID) assesses fees that are used to fund management and staff maintenance for the park.

People like the movable chairs in Bryant Park.

User/Use Analysis

Significant behavioral problems identified in several studies of the park led to the current redevelopment. The detailed study conducted by Nager and Wentworth in the early 1970s identified the core physical problems. Many of these were perceived safety concerns that kept people out of the park except during peak periods. From 1977-80, the author occupied a faculty office directly across the street from Bryant Park. He frequently used the park during lunch hours and on nice days, and also had students use the park as a way to evaluate urban parks. The park was a run-down, yet pleasant, retreat from the busy world of midtown Manhattan. One would watch drug dealers exchanging trades on the edge of the park, yet the central lawn was often a safe haven, especially during periods of heavy use. It was the sense of danger that led planners and landowners to redevelop the park.

Since the redesign, the amount of use and the diversity of users have clearly increased in the park. Park use has reportedly more than doubled since the redesign, and female use of the park is up considerably according to records kept by the managers (Thompson 1997: 33). A student in the CUNY environmental psychology program that had conducted the original 1976 study completed a post-occupancy evaluation in 1993, after some construction had been completed (Park 1993). Using behavioral observation and interview methods, the author found that increased visual and physical access resulted in people feeling safer using the park. The CUNY study found that much of the success was due more to increased maintenance and policing than physical design. It is clear, however, that the redesign is a magnet for users and contributes to the park's overall success. Continued observation, evaluation, programming, and redesign will be needed to keep the park functioning as a successful urban park.

Peer Reviews

Bryant Park has received a very favorable reception by the larger community of landscape architects and urban designers. It has received many national awards from organizations such as the American Society of Landscape Architects, the American Institute of Architects, and the Regional Plan Association (Thompson 1997: 34). It has been widely publicized in professional magazines and books. Bryant Park was selected by a distinguished jury assembled by Urban Initiatives in 1996 as one of the sixty public spaces in America that were most successful and flourishing (Longo 1996). In 1998 it received one of the first Exemplary Place Awards from the Environmental Design Research Association and the journal *Places*, awarded by a jury that included landscape architect Lawrence Halprin, architect Donlyn Lyndon, and social researcher Clare Cooper Marcus. Bryant Park has become one of the most publicized and heralded urban parks since Central Park in New York City, designed by Frederick Law Olmsted. Bryant Park has also enjoyed very favorable reviews in the popular press. According to Bill Thompson (Thompson 1997: 34), *Time* magazine named Bryant Park the "Best Design of 1992;" *New York* magazine called it a "touch of the Tuileries. . . . the perfect endorsement for restoring public space with private funds;" and the *New York Times* former architectural critic Paul Goldberger viewed the restored park "a monument of pure joy."

Criticism

The redesigned park has not been without critics. Some have expressed fear that the park has become privatized. With its redesign and upgrading and the addition of an expensive restaurant, Bryant Park has attracted an upscale clientele and has discouraged use by others, many of whom are lower-income and homeless people.

Bryant Park is fun for children.

Performances animate Bryant Park.

Urban designer Stephen Carr, environmental psychologist Leanne Rivlin, planner Andrew Stone, and the author raised a number of concerns before the redevelopment of the park took place (Carr et al. 1992). One critique was whether Bryant Park could accommodate all of these new activities and still serve as a place of retreat and relaxation for some of its users. Another issue related to who had ultimate control of public parks. In spring 1983, BPRC, in cooperation with the New York Public Library, entered into a 35-year agreement with the city parks department whereby BPRC was to be responsible for all aspects of the park's maintenance, management, and renovation under the supervision of the city's parks commissioner. Responding to the original cafe proposal and the management plan, Peter Berle, then president of the NYC Parks Council, stated:

> I'm concerned about taking public land, removing it from the protections of public park status and turning it over to a private entity. If you have a private entity running a public park, who is to say that you and I may not be the undesirables next year? (Carmody 1983: B3).

Fred Kent, director of Project for Public Spaces in New York City, has criticized Bryant Park more recently for its lack of success in becoming a true democratic open space:

> Even high-profile parks are showing signs of being in trouble. New York's Bryant Park—famed for a renovation that brought crowds to a once-derelict hangout for drug dealers—is one example. While its lush lawns and convenient moveable chairs make it a heavily used place for much of the year, it is increasingly given over to private interests. At the main park entrance, Starbucks has taken the place of local coffee purveyors. And the park is virtually inaccessible to regular folk for up to a month each year, due to the semi-annual Mercedes-Benz New York Fashion Week (including set up and recovery). Despite its innovative history, Bryant Park has become a victim of its own success and is cutting itself off from the public it ought to be serving (Kent 2003: 1).

Significance and Uniqueness of Project

Bryant Park has become a model for how to transform rundown historic urban parks into lively and successful public spaces. The private-public partnership used to redevelop Bryant Park has been widely heralded as one of the best ways to renew older urban open spaces in periods of declining public funding of parks and open spaces (Berens 1998).

Limitations

It is unclear if the early success enjoyed at Bryant Park can be sustained over the longer term. Recent declines in funding for maintenance and management of Bryant Park have caused some to worry whether current levels of use can be maintained without impacting the park's overall image and safety.

Generalizable Features and Lessons

The key ingredients of Bryant Park's rebirth—programming, movable seating, food, high quality maintenance, strong design and detailing—are now considered standard for any successful public open space. While the scale of funding used to transform Bryant Park was not typical, even in major parks in other downtown areas, there is evidence that funding is increasing for park rehabilitation. Bryant Park's process and design offers several lessons for the design of similar park projects. The process used in Bryant Park's transformation is a model for similar projects, demonstrating how behavioral analysis can be combined with thoughtful design to create successful public spaces. Yet not every urban park can command a multimillion-dollar budget raised from private sources. Most projects are more modest in budget and scope. However the principles are the same—get people involved, do careful social and economic analysis, realize that design alone is often not enough (programming and management are critical as well), and expect that successful parks must be continuously evaluated and redesigned to ensure success.

The Bryant Park Restoration Corporation is continually seeking additional funding for the park. They would like to extend the park hours and institute a sculpture program (Berens 1998). In addition they would like to renovate the Pavilion at the corner of West 40th Street and Sixth Avenue.

Participation is the process of working collaboratively with individuals and groups to achieve specific goals. Open spaces allow designers and public officials to directly involve their constituencies in the ongoing design, planning, and management of these resources

COMMUNITY PARTICIPATION

The process of community participation results in informed and engaged residents that feel better connected to their communities. While sometimes contentious, but more often productive and rewarding, community participation is an essential ingredient of making successful urban open space. Open spaces provide residents with a venue for participation in and attachment to their communities. They also provide a sense of place and offer essential life-enhancing qualities that aid community and individual well-being.

Urban open spaces can also create a sense of place by connecting residents to one another and to their larger environment. They can physically reconnect communities to themselves by creating linkages or restoring historic connections broken by highways, sprawl, and poor planning decisions. Greenways, green streets, and linear parks are now widely used open space types (Smith and Hellmund 1993).

The benefits of participation in the development of urban parks and open spaces include a stronger sense of community (PPS 2000) and an increased sense of user or community control (Francis 1989a). There are also many low cost and effective methods of community participation, such as workshops, surveys, interviews, and observation (Hester 1990).

OPPOSITE Participation is a good way to plan for user needs.

The historic Children's Garden at the Brooklyn Botanical Garden, New York City.

Yet participation does have risks and limits that need to be understood. Landscape architect Randy Hester suggests that participation sometimes leads to what he calls "participatory gridlock" where nothing is agreed upon or the resulting plans runs counter to established environmental or social goals. He suggests that participation, to be effective, needs to been done with "a view"—a clear vision on the part of the city officials and designers of the desired future (Hester 1999). While this vision can be modified and enlarged by participants during the design and planning process, the city officials and designers need to be proactive in their approach (Francis 1999).

A children's playground in lower Manhattan, New York City.

Mission Creek in San Luis Obispo, California, was saved from being channelized by the U.S. Army Corps of Engineers due to community opposition from local citizens.

THE LANDSCAPE ARCHITECT'S ROLE

Landscape architects play a critical and often decisive role in providing for user needs in open space projects. They can be influential in educating clients and listening to users to determine how spaces should be best designed. Landscape architects need to become more involved in the making of the public realm. Firms such as Hargreaves Associates, Olin Partnership, Ken Smith, and Field Operations have shown that landscape architects can be leaders in making public space by their redesign proposals for "Ground Zero" in Lower Manhattan. One way that design professionals can become more proactive is through better continuing education for professionals on best methods and practices and training for landscape students on how to incorporate user needs in design.

A transit shelter on the Portland Transit Mall in Oregon.

APPROACHES TO MAINTENANCE AND MANAGEMENT

How a space is managed and maintained has been found to be critical to its success. The art and science of managing public spaces is now well developed with numerous management techniques, including activity programming, user management groups and public-private partnerships. These methods have been effectively employed in the redesign of Bryant Park in New York City and Union Square in San Francisco. There are several guidebooks available that are useful in addressing user needs in the management of urban open spaces. Ways to assess human use and reduce user conflicts through management also include user analysis methods, adequate participation, and strong management.

Management can provide access to sunny places to sit such as this commercial street next to the University of Oregon campus in Eugene.

EVALUATING THE NEEDS AND LIMITATIONS OF PUBLIC SPACES

There have been significant advances in methods to identify user needs in public open spaces. Most significant is the use of post-occupancy evaluation (POE) as a way to assess if human use and design intentions are in fact successful (Cooper Marcus and Francis 1998). There are several methods that are most commonly used to identify issues of user needs and conflicts in open spaces.[10] They include archival research, observation, behavior mapping, interviews, environmental autobiography, mapping, participation, photography, aerial photo analysis, GIS, and CAD. Most past studies have used these methods in combination to study and design urban open spaces.

The Literature on User Needs in Urban Open Space

There is a large literature on user needs and conflicts in public space. Professional design magazines such as *Landscape Architecture* and *Places* feature articles and projects related to user needs and conflicts. Peer-reviewed research journals such as *Landscape Journal*, *Journal of Architectural and Planning Research*, and the *Journal of Urban Design* publish empirical studies of urban open spaces. In addition, some design awards programs such as the EDRA/Places Awards Program and the Rudy Bruner Award in Environmental Design specifically emphasize user needs in the design of urban places.[11] A more complete listing of journals is included at the end of this case study.

OPPOSITE A participatory fountain in Flint, Michigan.

---

10 / Madden and Love, *User Analysis: An Approach to Park Planning and Management* published by the Project for Public Spaces in 1982, is still one of the most comprehensive and useful. See also Zeisel, *Inquiry by Design* (2001).

11 / Most professional design award programs, such as those provided by the American Society of Landscape Architects and American Institute of Architects, do not require evidence of use and user satisfaction as criteria for design awards. Publications and descriptions of these award-winning projects are too often devoid of human use.

Critical Reviews

Some have argued that use alone does not make a well-designed open space. For example, Project for Public Spaces in New York City (2000) states that places should be created, "not just designed." Three of their "Eleven Steps to Transforming Public Spaces into Great Community Places" emphasize programming over design and the evolving nature of good open spaces. Furthermore they stress that a design is "never finished" (PPS 2000).

> If your goal is to create a place (which we think it should be), a design will not be enough. . . . The goal is to create a place that has both a strong sense of community and a comfortable image, as well as a setting and activities and uses that collectively add up to something more than the sum of its often-simple parts. This is easy to say, but difficult to accomplish. . . . Although design is important, these other elements tell you what "form" you need to accomplish the future vision for the space (PPS 2000).

Clearly, user need is only one of many considerations in open space design, but an important one. Other issues, such as budget, aesthetics, and form, are important but often are emphasized at the expense of user needs. What is required is more of an integrated approach to open space design where ecology, economics, technology, social and cultural concerns, and design all are combined in the making of open spaces. There also needs to be a more open-minded view of potential users that addresses the full range and diversity of possible users. This requires asking who is not using a site and how they can be attracted to use it.

A further problem is that community participation may lead some users to want designers to fence and alarm an open space, limit uses, and even users. Some scholars such as Louise Mozingo (1995) argue that landscape architects need to advocate for a larger public good, and that asking people what they want can lead to some problems. Users can sometimes be narrow-minded and selfish and do not concern themselves with the greater public good; therefore community process work can unfortunately be the means of making a public place less public.

There is also a need for more critical and outside reviews of open space projects to document successes and failures. *Landscape Architecture* has recently played a valuable role in this regard. Supporting evaluation and criticism is an important role for LAF's *Land and Community Design Case Studies.*

Playing Chess in Central Square, Bergen, Norway.

Why Design Urban Open Spaces?

User need is a significant issue in the successful design of open space. While there are other important issues, such as those discussed earlier, needs are often a prerequisite to addressing other issues. Although some needs are unique and can vary from space to space, there are some universal principles that can be applied to the design and redesign of urban parks and open spaces.

Limitations and Problems

One of the reasons commonly used by designers for not addressing the people needs in design is lack of time and budget. Yet many designers lack an understanding of research advances, leading to often-superficial design attention to user needs and conflicts. Additionally, designers and managers also often lack good methods of community outreach to inspire and guide user visioning and participation. Most clients are sensitive to these issues, and some do encourage designers to address them in the programming and participation process for projects. Other clients must be convinced that time spent on addressing user needs upfront can save money later on. The author's own design experience, as well as that of professionals such as Randy Hester, Tom Fox, and Susan Goltsman, has proven that while it may take some extra time to address user needs and conflicts early in the design process, this will save time later by avoiding project delays and the potential for future redesign.

A pedestrian park in Madrid, Spain.

Principles of Public Places

While some factors are specific to site and surrounding conditions, principles of user needs are common to most places. Dimensions such as comfort, relaxation, passive and active engagement, discovery, and fun are generalizable to the design of most urban open spaces. User conflicts based on culture, age, or gender are also common to most types of spaces. The Project for Public Spaces, through its research in the states and abroad, suggests a number of design techniques that can make successful public spaces. The Project for Public Spaces offers the following design and management recommendations for improving existing open spaces, as well as for the design of new open spaces, in Table 6.

TABLE 6

Design & Management Recommendations for Public Open Space

USES AND ACTIVITIES

— Provide amenities that will support desired activities.

— Create focal points where people gather.

— Develop a series of community-oriented programs with local talent from institutions (churches, schools, libraries, farmers markets, and so forth) to attract people in the short term and to demonstrate that someone is in charge.

— Change the type of events that are held or modify the space, if necessary, to better accommodate events.

— Work with adjacent property owners and retailers to develop strategies to lease ground floors of empty buildings and help revitalize the area.

COMFORT AND IMAGE

— Add practical amenities—seating, telephones, waste receptacles, information booths, food vendors, community-oriented public art, flowers, fountains—in carefully considered locations.

— Create a management presence through vendors or food and information kiosks by creating an entrance or adding a view onto the place from windows in an adjacent building.

— Increase security by providing more uses for and activities at the place, which will increase the number of people present, or by appointing an individual to be in charge of security.

— Upgrade maintenance, including daily cleaning, and preventive maintenance of physical facilities.

— Establish a community-policing program.

ACCESS AND LINKAGES

— Widen sidewalks or provide sidewalk extensions at crosswalks, better balancing pedestrian uses with other uses (vehicles, transit vehicles, bicycles, deliveries, and so forth).

— Construct clearly marked and/or conveniently located crosswalks.

— Make accommodations for bicycle users (bike lanes, lockers, storage racks, etc.).

— Infill vacant lots with structures and uses to create continuity of pedestrian experience.

— Balance on-street parking with other uses.

— Change traffic signal timing to improve pedestrian access.

— Improve use of parking through changes in enforcement or regulation.

SOCIABILITY

— Develop focal points—public gathering places that accommodate a variety of activities.

— Arrange amenities to encourage social interaction, such as grouped benches and movable seating.

— Stage special events and activities to draw people.

— Encourage community volunteers to assist with improvements or maintenance of a place.

— Provide a variety of uses in adjacent building to attract a diversity of people.

Source: Project for Public Spaces, *How to Turn a Place Around*, 2000, 86–93.

A sculpture park in Madrid, Spain.

Harborplace in Baltimore, Maryland.

Issues and Research for the Future

With all the advances in research and practice in user needs in open space, several significant issues remain. Most notable is the need for a better understanding of the role of design in addressing user needs in parks and open spaces. A larger number of case studies of real places where design has attempted to address user needs is required.

Future research needs in this area include:

• The role of history and theory in addressing user needs and conflicts in open space.[12]

• The effect of citizen activism and participation (including NIMBYism) on the creation, use, and experience of open space.

• Economic costs and benefits of providing for user needs.

• Plant selection that addresses users needs.

• The effect of sustainable practices and design on user needs.

• The differences and similarities of user, designer, and manager aesthetics of public spaces.

• Additional case studies of project success and failure as well as best practices that address user needs.

Other useful approaches include creating the programming for the public space early on, and making this part of the program elements of the design. Designers and public space developers need to coordinate with one another; user participation is especially effective at this stage. The use of existing design patterns can also inform design. A good deal of information on successful design elements is available from the Urban Parks Institute, City Parks Forum, and Trust for Public Land (see References for contact information). Pattern books such as Christopher Alexander et al. *A Pattern Language* (1977) are helpful sources and should be carefully modified to fit each context and situation.

---

12 / Galen Cranz's *The Politics of Park Design* (1982), provides a useful historical analysis that shows how concern for user needs changed significantly during the 20th century. See also Hayden, *Power of Place* (1995), and Birnbaum and Karson, *Pioneers of American Landscape Design* (2000).

CONCLUSIONS AND RECOMMENDATIONS

Designing for human needs will continue to pose significant challenges for open space designers and managers. Increased understanding of both needs and conflicts and their role in urban open space development will be required in the future. Designers need to distinguish between accounting for user needs in two different circumstances.[13] One situation is where there are existing constituents to observe and work with such as redesigning an existing public space; the second is where the involved constituents will not necessarily be the ultimate users. Here research on user needs is particularly helpful. In some public open spaces a community design process is more helpful than literature-based research; in others, research may be more useful.

Past case studies suggest that open spaces—even good ones—cannot just be designed and forgotten. They need to be evaluated and redesigned over time to address changing user needs. Post-occupancy evaluation (POE) in the form of case studies should become an integral part of all built open spaces. Public park agencies, nonprofit organizations, citizen groups, and landscape architects, such as local chapters of ASLA, should form partnerships to support this kind of ongoing evaluation and redesign in their communities. They should not be isolated studies, but should become part of larger comprehensive open space programs.

OPPOSITE Downtown San Francisco is a vibrant urban space.

13 / The author is grateful to Louise Mozingo for pointing out this fundamental difference.

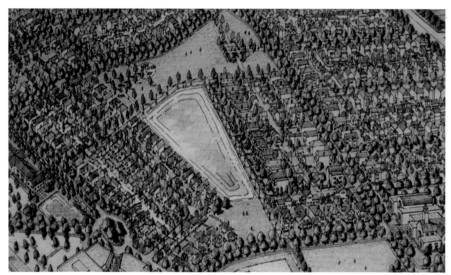

New Urbanist plans need to consider user needs and conflicts in their design.

Organizations like the Landscape Architecture Foundation, along with the American Society of Landscape Architects and sister organizations such as the Trust for Public Land, Urban Land Institute, City Parks Forum, and Urban Parks Institute, can partner to address user needs and conflicts in open space. This is an issue too large for any one group to address alone, and such partnerships can shed new light on best principles and practices for open space preservation and development. It appears that there will be increased public support and potentially greater funding to support such efforts.

EMU Plaza at the University of Oregon, an example of a well-designed open space that includes user needs.

Directions for Future Work

Public interest and support will continue to expand for the preservation and development of urban open space. Landscape architects will need to find ways to play a more central leadership role in this growing national and local movement. To do so, they need to better use research advances in their design work. In addition, researchers must close gaps in their understanding of user needs such as the appropriate role of design and form in making comfortable and memorable places for people. Case studies are an effective way their influence can be expanded and projects made more successful. Continued research in the form of new case studies is needed to show how user needs can be effectively translated into design. Programming, planning, design, and management based on human needs will be essential to the future development of open spaces as well as the growth of the profession.

BIBLIOGRAPHY

Adams, E. 1990. *Learning Through Landscapes.* UK: Learning through Landscapes Trust.

Altman, I., and E. Zube, eds. 1989. Public Places and Spaces. *Human Behavior and Environment,* Vol. 10. New York: Plenum.

Arreola, D. 1995. Urban Ethnic Landscape Identity. *Geographical Review* 85, 4: 518–534.

August, M. 2000. Today's Political Landscape, Land. *ASLA.* December 1.

Barlow, B. 1987. *Rebuilding Central Park: A Management and Restoration Plan.* Cambridge: MIT Press.

Becker, F. 1973. A Class-conscious Evaluation: Going back to Sacramento's Pedestrian Mall. *Landscape Architecture* 64: 295–345.

Bedard, M. 2000. Healthy Landscapes: Guidelines for Therapeutic City Form. Unpublished Master's Thesis, University of California, Davis.

Berens, G. 1997. Bryant Park. *Urban Parks and Open Space.* Washington, DC: The Urban Land Institute: 44–57.

Beveridge, C. E., D. Larkin, and P. Rocheleau. 1995. *Frederick Law Olmsted: Designing the American Landscape.* New York: Rizzoli.

Birnbaum, C. A., and R. A. Karson,eds. 2000. *Pioneers of American Landscape Design.* New York: McGraw Hill.

Bosselmann, P. 1983. Shadowboxing: Keeping Sunlight on Chinatown's Kids. *Landscape Architecture* 73: 74–76.

Briffet, C. 2001. Is Managed Recreational Use Compatible with Effective Habitat and Wildlife Occurrence in Urban Open Space Corridor Systems? *Landscape Research* 26, 2: 137–163.

Brower, S. 1988. *Design in Familiar Places.* New York: Praeger.

———.1996. *Good Neighborhoods.* New York: Praeger.

Bunston, T., and M. Breton. 1992. Homes and Homeless Women. *Journal of Environmental Psychology* 12: 149–162.

Calthorpe, P. 1993. *The Next American Metropolis: Ecology, Community, and the American Dream.* New York: Princeton Architectural Press.

Carmody, D. 1983. Proposal for Restaurant in Bryant Park Disputed. *The New York Times.* May 16: B3.

Carr, S., M. Francis, L. Rivlin, and A. Stone. 1992. *Public Space.* New York: Cambridge University Press.

Carr, S., and K. Lynch. 1981. Open Space: Freedom and Control. In L. Taylor, *Urban Open Spaces.* New York: Rizzoli.

Chidister, M. 1986. The Effect of Context on the use of Urban Plazas. *Landscape Journal* 5, 2: 115–127.

Cochran, A., M. Francis, and H. Schenker,eds. 1998. 35 *Case Studies of California Urban Parks.* Davis, CA: Center for Design Research.

Colorado State Trails Program. 1995. The Effect of Greenways on Property Values and Public Safety.

Cooper, C. 1970. Adventure Playgrounds. *Landscape Architecture* 61, 1:18–29, 88–91.

Cooper Marcus, C. and M. Barnes, eds. 1999. *Healing Gardens.* New York: Wiley.

Cooper Marcus, C., and C. Francis, eds. 1998. *People Places: Design Guidelines for Urban Open Space.* Second Edition. New York: Wiley.

Cooper Marcus, C., and T. Wischemann. 1987. Outdoor Spaces for Living and Learning. *Landscape Architecture* 78: 54–61.

Cranz, G. 1982. *The Politics of Park Design.* Cambridge: MIT Press.

Flink, C., and R. Searns. 1993. *Greenways, A Guide to Planning, Design, and Development.* Washington, DC: Island Press.

Fox, T. 1990. *Urban Open Space: An Investment that Pays.* New York: Neighborhood Open Space Coalition.

Fox, T., I. Koeppel, and S. Kellam. 1985. *Struggle for Space: The Greening of New York City.* New York: Neighborhood Open Space Coalition.

Francis, M. 1987a. Urban Open Spaces. In E. Zube and G. Moore, eds. *Advances in Environment, Behavior and Design.* New York: Plenum.

———.1987b. The Making of Democratic Streets. In A. Vernez-Moudon, ed., *Public Streets For Public Use.* New York: Columbia University Press.

———.1987c. Some Different Meanings Attached to a Public Park and Community Gardens. *Landscape Journal* 6: 100–112.

———. 1988. Changing Values for Public Space. *Landscape Architecture* 78, 1: 54–59. January–February.

———. 1989a. *Control as a Dimension of Public Space Quality.* In I. Altman and E. Zube, eds., *Public Places and Spaces. Human Behavior and Environment.* Volume 10. New York: Plenum.

———. 1989b. The Urban Garden as Public Space. *Places* 6, l.

———. 1999a. A Case Study Method for Landscape Architecture. Final Report. Washington, DC: Landscape Architecture Foundation.

———. 1999b. Proactive Practice: Visionary Thought and Participatory Action in Environmental Design. *Places* 12, 1: 60–68.

———. 1999c. Making a Community's Place. In R. Hester and C. Kweskin, eds., *Democratic Design in the Pacific Rim: Japan, Taiwan and U.S.* Mendocino, CA: Ridge Times Press: 156–163.

———. 2000a. A Case Study Method for Landscape Architecture. *Landscape Journal* 19, 2.

———. 2000b. Habits of the Proactive Practitioner. In I. Kinoshita, ed., Proceedings of the Second Conference of Democratic Design in the Pacific Rim: Japan, Taiwan and U. S. Tokyo.

———. 2001. *Village Homes: A Place-Based Case Study.* Washington DC: Landscape Architecture Foundation.

———. 2002. Village Homes: A Case Study in Community Design. *Landscape Journal.* 21, 1: 23–41.

———. 2003. Parks as Community Engagement: A Guide for Mayors. Chicago: City Parks Forum, American Planning Association.

Francis, M., and C. Bowns. 2001. Research-Based Design of an Urban Wildlife Preserve. In J. Zeisel, *Inquiry by Design.* Second Edition. New York: Cambridge University Press.

Francis, M., L. Cashdan, and L. Paxson. 1984. *Community Open Spaces.* Washington, DC: Island Press.

Franck, K. A. and L. Paxson. 1989. Women and Urban Public Space: Research, Design, and Policy Issues. In E. Zube and G. Moore, eds, *Advances in Environment, Behavior and Design,* Vol. 2. New York: Plenum: 122–146.

Garvin, A., and G. Berens. 1997. *Urban Parks and Open Spaces.* Washington: The Urban Land Institute.

Gehl, J.1987. *The Life Between Buildings.* New York: Van Nostrand Reinhold.

Gehl, J. and L. Gemoze. 1996. *Public Spaces Public Life.* Copenhagen: Danish Architectural Press.

Girling, C. L., and K. Helphand. 1994. *Yard, Street, Park: The Design of Suburban Open Space.* New York: Wiley.

Gobster, P.H., and B. Hull. 2000. *Restoring Nature.* Washington, DC: Island Press.

Gobster, P. H., and L. M. Westphal. 1995. *People and the River.* Chicago: USDA Forest Service, North Central Forest Experiment Station.

Gold, S. M. 1972. Nonuse of Neighborhood Parks. *Journal of the American Planning Association* 38, 6: 369–378.

Goltsman, S., D. Iacofano, and R. Moore. 1987. *The Play for All Guidelines: Planning, Design and Management of Outdoor Settings for All Children.* Berkeley: MIG Communications.

Hamilton, L. W., ed. 1997. T*he Benefits of Open Space.* Trenton: Rutgers University and Great Swamp Watershed Association.

Harnik, P. 2000. *Inside City Parks.* Washington DC: Urban Land Institute.

Hart, R. A. 1978. *Children's Experience of Place.* New York: Irvington.

———. 1997. *Children's Participation.* New York: UNICEF.

Hayden, D. 1995. *The Power of Place.* Cambridge: MIT Press.

Hester, R. T., Jr. 1975. *Planning Neighborhood Spaces with People.* New York: Dowden Hutchinson & Ross.

———. 1983. Labors of Love in the Public Landscape. *Places* 1: 18–27.

———. 1985. Subconscious Landscapes in the Heart. *Places* 2, 10–22.

———. 1990. *Community Design Primer.* Ridge Times Press.

———. 1999. Refrain With a View. *Places.*

Hester, R. T., Jr., N. J. Blazej, and I. S. Moore. 2000. Whose Wild? Resolving Cultural and Biological Diversity Conflicts in Urban Wilderness. *Landscape Journal* 18, 2: 137–146.

Hester, R., and C. Kweskin, eds. 1999. *Democratic Design in the Pacific Rim: Japan, Taiwan and U.S.* Mendocino, CA: Ridge Times Press.

Hiss, T. 1990. *The Experience of Place.* New York: Knopf.

Holloway, S., and G. Valentine, eds. 2000. *Children's Geographies: Living, Playing, Learning and Transforming Everyday Worlds.* London: Routledge.

Hood, W. 1997. *Urban Diaries.* Washington, DC: Spacemaker Press.

Hough, M. 1995. *Cities and Natural Process.* New York: Routledge.

Jacobs, A. 1995. *Great Streets.* Cambridge: MIT Press.

Jacobs, J. 1961. *The Death and Life of Great American Cities.* New York: Vintage Books.

Johnson, J. 2000. Design for Learning: Values, Qualities and Processes of Enriching School Landscapes. LATIS Document. Washington, DC: American Society of Landscape Architects.

Joardar, S. D., and J. W. Neill. 1978. The Subtle Difference in Configuration of Small Public Place. *Landscape Architecture* 68,

11: 487–491.

Jones, S. [forthcoming]. Open Space and Environmental Equity. *Landscape Journal.*

Jones, S., and A. Graves. 2000. Power Plays in Public Space: Skateboards as Battle Ground, Gifts, and Expressions of Self. *Landscape Journal* 19, 1, 2: 136–148.

Jones, S., and P. Welch. 1999. Evolving Visions: Segregation, Integration, and Inclusion in the Design of Built Places. *Proceedings of the Environmental Design Research Association* [EDRA]. EDRA 30.

Kaplan, R. and S. Kaplan. 1989. *The Experience of Nature.* New York: Cambridge University Press.

Kaplan, R., S. Kaplan, and R. L. Ryan. 1998. *With People in Mind: Design and Management of Everyday Nature.* Washington, DC: Island Press.

Karasov, D., ed. 1993. *The Once and Future Park.* New York: Princeton Architectural Press.

Kayden, J. S. 2000. *Privately Owned Public Space: The New York City Experience.* New York: Wiley.

Kent, F. 2003. Urban Parks: Innovate Or Stagnate. Op Ed. *Planetizen.* New York: Project for Public Spaces.

Kepes, G., ed. 1972. *Arts of the Environment.* New York: George Braziller.

Kinoshita, I., ed. 2000. Proceedings of the Second Conference of Democratic Design in the Pacific Rim: Japan, Taiwan and U. S. Tokyo.

Kretzman, J. P., and J. L. McKnight. 1993. *Building Communities From the Inside Out: A Path Toward Finding and Mobilizing a Community's Assets.* Evanston IL: Center for Urban Affairs and Policy Research, Neighborhood Innovations Network, Northwestern University.

Lewis, C. 1996. *Green Nature/Human Nature: The Meaning of Plants in Our Lives.* Urbana: University of Illinois Press.

Lindsay, N. 1977. Drawing Socio-Economic Lines in Central Park. *Landscape Architecture* 67, 6: 515–520.

Lofland, L. 1998. *The Public Realm: Exploring the City's Quintessential Social Territory.* New York: Aldine De Gruyter.

Longo, G. 1996. *Great American Public Places.* New York: Urban Initiatives.

Loukaitou-Sideris, A. 1995. Urban Form and Social Context: Cultural Differentiation in the Uses of Urban Parks. *Journal of Planning Education and Research* 14, 2: 89–102.

Love, R.L. 1973. *The Fountains of Urban Life.* Urban Life and Culture 2: 161–209.

Lynch, K. 1972. The Openness of Open Space. In G. Kepes, ed., *Arts of the Environment.* New York: George Braziller.

———. 1981. *Good City Form.* Cambridge: MIT Press.

Mitchell, D. 1998. Anti-Homeless Laws and Public Space: Begging and the First Amendment. *Urban Geography* 19, 2: 98–104.

Madden, K., and K. Love. 1982. *User Analysis: An Approach to Park Planning and Management.* New York: Project for Public Spaces.

Moore, R. C. 1993. *Plants for Play: A Plant Selection Guide for Children's Outdoor Environments.* Berkeley: MIG Communications.

Moore, R. C. 1986. *Childhood's Domain: Play and Place in Child Development.* London: Croom-Helm.

Moore, R. C., and H. H. Wong. 1997. *Natural Learning: The Life History of an Environmental Schoolyard.* Berkeley: MIG Communications.

Mozingo, L. 1989. Women and Downtown Open Space. *Places* 6, 1, Fall.

———. 1995. Public Space in the Balance. *Landscape Architecture.* February.

Nager, A. R., and W. R. Wentworth. 1976. [1977 in text] *Bryant Park: A Comprehensive Evaluation of its Image and Use with Implications for Urban Open Space Design.* New York: CUNY Center for Human Environments.

Newman, O. 1973. *Defensible Space.* New York: MacMillian.

Nicholson, S. 1971. Theory of Loose Parts: How Not to Cheat Children. *Landscape Architecture* 62: 30–34.

Oldenburg, R. 1989. *The Great Good Place.* New York: Paragon.

Owens, P. E. 1998. Natural Landscapes, Gathering Places, and Prospect Refuges: Characteristics of Outdoor Places Valued by Teens. *Children's Environments Quarterly* 5, 2: 17–24.

Parks Council. 1993. *Public Space for Public Life: A Plan for the 21st Century.* New York: The Parks Council and Central Park Conservancy.

Phillips, L. E. 1996. Parks: *Design and Management.* New York: McGraw Hill.

Project for Public Spaces (PPS). 2000. *How To Turn a Place Around.* New York: PPS.

Rivlin, L.G. 1986 [1996 in text]. A New Look at the Homeless. *Social Policy* 16, 4: 3–10.

Rowe, P. G. 1997. *Civic Realism.* Cambridge: The MIT Press.

Sandels, S. 1975. *Children in Traffic.* London: Paul Elek.

Schwartz, L., C. Flink, and R. Stearns. 1993. *Greenways: A Guide to Planning, Design, and Development.* Washington, DC: Island Press.

Seamon, D., and C. Nordon. 1980. Marketplace as Place Ballet: A Swedish example. *Landscape* 24: 35–41.

Sommer, R. Farmers Markets as Community Events. 1989. In I. Altman and E. Zube, eds., *Public Places and Spaces.* New York: Plenum: 57–82.

Sommer, R. and F. Becker. 1969. The Old Men in Plaza Park. *Landscape Architecture* 59: 111–113.

Spirn, A. 1999. *The Language of Landscape.* New Haven: Yale.

Stine, S. 1997. *Landscapes for Learning.* New York: Wiley.

Taylor, L. 1981. *Urban Open Spaces.* New York: Rizzoli.

Taylor, A. F., F. E. Kuo, and W. C. Sullivan. 2001. Coping With ADD: The Surprising Connection to Green Play Settings. *Environment and Behavior* 33, 1: 54 –77.

Thompson, W. 1997. *The Rebirth of New York City's Bryant Park.* Washington, DC: Spacemaker Press.

Tishler, W., ed. 1989. *American Landscape Architecture.* Washington, DC: National Trust for Historic Preservation.

Trust for Public Land (TPL). 1994. *Healing America's Cities: Why We Must Invest in Urban Parks.* San Francisco: TPL.

Ulrich, R. S. 1981. Natural Versus Urban Scenes: Some Psychophysiological Effects. *Environment and Behavior* 13: 523–555.

———. 1984. View Through a Window May Influence Recovery from Surgery. *Science* 224: 420–421.

Ulrich, R., and D. L. Addoms. 1981. Psychological and Recreational Benefits of a Residential Park. *Journal of Leisure Research* 13, 1: 43–65.

Vernez-Moudon, A., ed. 1987. *Public Streets for Public Use.* New York: Columbia University Press.

Warner, S. B. 1987. *To Dwell is to Garden.* Boston: Northeastern University Press.

Whyte, W. H. 1979. Revitalization of Bryant Park. Report to the Rockefeller Brothers Fund.

———. 1980. *The Social Life of Small Urban Spaces.* Washington, DC: The Conservation Foundation.

———. 1988. *City: Rediscovering the Center.* New York: Doubleday.

Zeisel, J. 2001. *Inquiry by Design.* Second Edition. New York: Cambridge University Press.

Zube, E. and G. Moore, eds. 1987. *Advances in Environment, Behavior and Design.* New York: Plenum.

JOURNALS

Architecture

*Children's Environment Quarterly**

Harvard Design Journal

Journal of American Planning Association

Journal of Architectural & Planning Research

Journal of Urban Design

*Landscape**

Landscape Architecture

Landscape & Urban Planning

Landscape Journal

Places

* These journals are no longer in print, but their back issues contain useful articles and studies on user needs and conflicts.

WEBSITES AND LISTSERVS

Adaptive Environments: www.adaptenv.org

American Community Gardening Association: www.communitygarden.org

American Planning Association: www.planning.org

Council of Educators in Landscape Architecture: www.ssc.msu.edu/~la/cela/

Environmental Design Research Association: www.edra.org

Landscape Architecture Foundation: www.LAFoundation.org

Project for Public Spaces: www.pps.org

Trust for Public Land: www.tpl.org

University of Toronto CLIP site: www.clr.utoronto.ca/virtuallib/clip

Urban Land Institute: www.uli.org

Urban Parks Institute: www.pps.org/urbanparks

PHOTO CREDITS

SOURCES OF INFORMATION

American Society of Landscape
Architects (ASLA)
636 Eye Street, NW
Washington, DC 20001<KKIAUj3736
202-898-2444
202-898-1185 FAX
www.asla.org

CLIP: Contemporary Landscape
Inquiry Project
Center for Landscape Research
InterNetwork
School of Architecture and Landscape
Architecture
University of Toronto
230 College Street, Toronto, ON M5S
1A1
416-978-6788
wright@clr.utoronto.ca
www.clr.utoronto.ca/VIRTUALLIB/CLIP/

Environmental Design Research
Association
P.O. Box 7146
Edmond, OK 73083-7146
405-330-4863
405-330-4150 FAX
edra@telepath.com
www.telepath.com/edra/home.html

Landscape Architecture Foundation
818 18th Street, NW
Suite 810
Washington, DC 20006
202-331-7070
202-331-7079 FAX
www.LAFoundation.org

Project for Public Spaces (PPS)
153 Waverly Place, 4th floor
New York, NY 10014
212-620-5660
212-620-3821 FAX
pps@pps.org
www.pps.org

Trust for Public Land (TPL)
116 New Montgomery St., 4th Floor
San Francisco, CA 94105
415-495-4014
415-495-4103 FAX
info@tpl.org
www.tpl.org

Urban Land Institute Project
Reference Files
1025 Thomas Jefferson St, NW
Suite 500 W
Washington, DC 20007-5201
202-624-7016
202-624-7140 FAX
www.uli.org/prf/test/index.htm

Urban Parks Institute (UPI)
153 Waverly Place, 4th floor
New York, NY 10014
212-620-5660
212-620-3821 FAX
Urbparks@pps.org
www.pps.org/urbanparks

INDEX

ABOUT THE AUTHOR

Mark Francis, a Fellow of the American Society of Landscape Architects, is professor of landscape architecture at the University of California, Davis, and senior design consultant with Moore Iacofano Goltsman. Trained in landscape architecture and urban design at Berkeley and Harvard, he is author of more than sixty articles and book chapters translated into a dozen languages. His books include *Community Open Spaces* (Island, 1984), *The Meaning of Gardens* (MIT, 1990), *Public Space* (Cambridge, 1992), and *The California Landscape Garden: Ecology, Culture and Design* (California, 1999). He has received eight Honor and Merit awards and a Centennial Medallion from the American Society of Landscape Architects for his design, planning, research, and writing. His work has focused on the use and meaning of the built and natural landscape. Much of this research has utilized a case study approach to study parks, gardens, public spaces, streets, nearby nature, and urban public life. He is past president of the Environmental Design Research Association, is associate editor of the *Journal of Architectural & Planning Research* and serves on the editorial boards of *Landscape Journal, Journal of Planning Literature, Environment & Behavior, Children's and Youth Environments,* and *Design-Research Connections.*

AUTHOR ACKNOWLEDGMENTS

This case study follows a methodology and format developed previously for the Landscape Architecture Foundation (LAF). This is one of three prototype case studies (place-based, issue-based and teaching) developed by the author for LAF's *Land and Community Design Case Study Series.* It is intended both as an issue-based case study of user needs in urban open spaces and as a prototype case study that will aid others in developing issue-oriented cases of designed landscapes.

The preparation of this case study was aided by the Ralph Hudson Environmental Fellowship from the CLASS Fund and the Graham Foundation for Advanced Studies in the Fine Arts. In addition, support was provided by the University of California Agricultural Experiment Station. I would also like to thank Mary Bedard, Kathy Blaha, Susan Everett, Tom Fox, Peter Harnik, Randy Hester, Stanton Jones, Lyn Lofland, Louise Mozingo, and Leanne Rivlin, and Frederick Steiner who provided helpful comments and suggestions for this case study, as well as the anonymous reviewers who provided useful comments on an earlier version.

I am grateful to the LAF and its board for commissioning this study and for their overall support of the case study initiative in landscape architecture. I would especially like to thank Frederick Steiner, former LAF president and dean at the University of Texas in Austin, and LAF executive director Susan Everett for their assistance and encouragement. I would like to express my gratitude to Heather Boyer at Island Press and Jan Cigliano for helping bringing this case study to a larger audience.

LANDSCAPE ARCHITECTURE FOUNDATION ACKNOWLEDGMENTS

Major support to LAF and its programs is provided by the American Society of Landscape Architects, ValleyCrest Landscape Development, Landscape Forms, Landscape Structures, Sasaki Associates, The Brickman Group, EDAW, Design Workshop, The HOK Planning Group, JJR, Canterbury International, LM Scofield Company, ONA, The Saratoga Associates and Robert Bristol, Civitas, Scott Byron and Company, Hunter Industries, Cold Spring Granite Company, EDSA, Sitecraft, Laurance S. Rockefeller, and the Bomanite Corporation.

Lead donors offering support to LAF programs include Burton Associates, Lannert Group, Dura Art Stone, Wyss Associates, Estrada Land Planning, NUVIS, Wallace Roberts & Todd, Carol R. Johnson Associates, Leatzow & Associates, Kim Lighting, The Toro Company Irrigation Division, SWA Group, LDR International, Glatting Jackson Kercher Anglin Lopez Rinehart, The Care of Trees, Signe Nielsen, Nimrod Long and Associates, Hughes, Good, O'Leary & Ryan, dhm design corporation, Hargreaves Associates, Meisner + Associates Land Vision, Peter Walker & Partners, Smith & Hawken, and other donors.

The Graham Foundation for Advanced Studies in the Fine Arts provided generous support at a critical juncture in the development of the case studies. We are deeply indebted to the Graham Foundation and its executive director, Richard Solomon, for their sage advice and early support.

LAF commissioned Mark Francis to develop the *Case Study Method in Landscape Architecture* in 1997, and subsequently, to write the prototypes for each of the case study types: project-based, issue-based and teaching. In the *Case Study Method in Landscape Architecture*, Mark went beyond merely creating a format for future case study researchers, creating in addition an ambitious vision for the program. We are grateful to Mark for the scope of his vision, his commitment, persistence, and leadership on the cases study series.

Mark Francis developed the case study series concept with the intent of creating an online archive of case study abstracts; case study compendia organized by type; case study institutes organized by project type or geographic region; sessions at annual meetings to focus on the case study method, comparative analysis, and theory building; and eventually, as the series develops, a national archive of case study projects related to the built and natural environment; a national conference on case studies that brings together national organizations; and public policy symposia that link case study findings to public policy issues.

The *Land & Community Design Case Study Series* National Advisory Council helped to shape the series during its formation. Our thanks to members Kathleen A. Blaha, L. Susan Everett, Mark Francis, Richard S. Hawks, Joe A. Porter, William H. Roberts, George L. Sass, Frederick R. Steiner, and Joanne M. Westphal. Vice president for information and research Gary A. Hack provided oversight and shaped the series as it evolved, and was instrumental in identifying and selecting a publishing partner. Frederick R. Steiner served as the vice president for information and research during the gestation of the case study series and as LAF president during a critical stage in its development. We appreciate his ongoing participation and guidance. The LAF California Landscape Architectural Student Scholarship Fund, known as the CLASS Fund, AILA Yamagami Hope Fellowship, supported the publication by LAF of the *Case Study Method in Landscape Architecture*.

The CLASS Fund supported the research for the issue-based prototype, *Urban Open Space*, through the Ralph Hudson Environmental Fellowship.

LAF wishes to thank the anonymous reviewers for their thoughtful comments and guidance, and the peer reviewers who provided insights and suggestions to each of the authors.

To produce the actual books, art director Mihae Kim and the design staff of the Gimga Group worked patiently with LAF on the graphic design as the series concept evolved, and supplied the creative design that gives the series its distinctively elegant appearance. Academy Press publisher and editor Jan Cigliano provided skilled organization and timely project management in working with the authors, publisher, graphic designer, and LAF on three publications simultaneously.

Heather Boyer, Island Press editor, graciously offered support and counsel throughout the development of the case study series and we are indebted to her for her invaluable and ongoing assistance. Island Press publisher and vice president Dan Sayre offered encouragement from the beginning and was willing to take a risk on a highly visual publication.